THE HISTORY OF 97 ORCHARD STREET AND THE LOWER EAST SIDE TENEMENT MUSEUM

Family in a tenement hallway, 1930s.

A Greek immigrant family,
Broome Street, c.1936.

The Lower East Side Tenement Museum thanks the American Express Company for making this publication possible.

ISBN 0-9749172-0-6
Published by the
Lower East Side Tenement Museum
90 Orchard Street,
New York, New York 10002
WWW.TENEMENT.ORG

Located in our country's most renowned immigrant neighborhood, the Lower East Side Tenement Museum interprets historic immigrant experiences to illuminate the present. By stimulating dialogue on pressing social issues to promote humanitarian and democratic values, the Museum has established a new model for the museum and preservation professions.

Josephine and Johnny Baldizzi on the roof of 97 Orchard Street, with a neighbor's child, c. 1935.

PART I FOUNDING A MUSEUM

ONE

Years flew by. Decades came and went. And each time Josephine Baldizzi Esposito visited the Lower East Side to shop, she'd walk by her childhood home at 97 Orchard Street filled with a sense of yearning, a longing to revisit her past.

"It was one of my dreams to get back into that house," she said of the tenement where her family lived from 1928 until 1935, when all the building's residents were evicted. For half a century, the tenement's dark, tiny apartments had remained shuttered and empty, casualties of New York City's increasingly stringent housing regulations. So Esposito was shocked when in 1989 she learned that her former home had been reborn as the Lower East Side Tenement Museum, a non-profit institution honoring the trials and triumphs of poor and unheralded families like her own. "It was unbelievable," she recalled.

Josephine Baldizzi standing outside the front door to her former apartment in 97 Orchard Street, 1993.

For Esposito, who lived in Brooklyn until her death in 1998, returning to 97 Orchard Street was "a dream come true." Her homecoming was also a stroke of good fortune for the Museum, which at its inception had planned to use fictional composites of immigrant families to bring the tenement experience to life. Inspired in part by Esposito's connection to 97 Orchard Street, where she lived from ages 2 through 9, the Museum eventually changed course.

Relying on Esposito's memories and a store of family artifacts, the Museum recreated the Baldizzi apartment as it had been in 1935: morning glories decorate window boxes that once held Home Relief provisions; her mother's pink shawl drapes an armchair; and rosary beads hang from a bureau. In 1994, the Museum unveiled the newly restored apartment as part of its first guided tenement tour. When Esposito saw her resurrected apartment, she said, "I felt like I'd gone back in time and was a little kid again."

Returning to 97 Orchard Street not only touched Esposito, it helped reawaken memories of her parents' brave and arduous journey from Palermo, Sicily, to America. Born and raised in New York, Esposito had grown distant from the experiences of her parents, and of newer immigrant groups. Revisiting 97 Orchard Street as both home and museum helped change that.

"When I came in contact with immigrants coming here now," Esposito says, "I would say, 'Oh my God, what country am I in? These are all foreign people. What are they all doing here?' Then I realized that these poor immigrants now are doing the same things my parents did."

TWO

It was precisely this type of understanding that Museum Founder and President Ruth J. Abram hoped to foster when she conceived of the Lower East Side Tenement Museum. Abram was not your typical museum founder: she was not a scholar intent on unearthing the minutiae of the past, nor was she a preservationist intrigued by the neighborhood's architecture.

Abram had been a social, civil rights and feminist activist before hitting upon the idea for the Tenement Museum. She then earned a master's degree in American history and gradually began developing the Museum with an eye toward nurturing a greater appreciation of groups often ethnically, economically and religiously divided.

African immigrants at Ellis Island at the turn of the century.

Chinese school children, 1910.

opposite, Joyce Mendelsohn, Museum educator, teaches a school group visiting the Tenement Museum.

When the Lower East Side Tenement Museum opened in 1988, Abram declared that it would "stand as a vibrant beacon for tolerance."

She viewed the tenement as the ideal place in which to encourage discussions of issues key to our democracy and national identity. "For a nation of immigrants, there is no single site more historically significant than the tenement," she says.

Ruth J. Abram
President and Founder,
Lower East Side
Tenement Museum.

The preservation and restoration of 97 Orchard Street is important not because the building once housed someone famous, but because this urban log cabin and its residents were so "ordinary": nearly 7,000 people from over 20 countries lived here between 1863 and 1935. In 1900, nearly three-quarters of New York City's population lived in tenements. The Lower East Side Tenement Museum, therefore, represents the masses, whose stories are at once personal and universal. And these tales are integral to understanding the development of America.

The Museum is devoted to bringing together people with divergent views. It is a response to those who argue that strong ethnic and religious identities interfere with assimilation and must be abandoned, as well as those who believe Old World ties are essential to survival. "The tenement building allows us to enter that debate," Abram said. "Behind every door is a family with a different religion, a different language, each unique.

The Museum in 1995.

But in the hallways, stoops, and streets, all those people are together pursuing the American Dream."

Abram hoped to motivate all visitors "to consider what programs, policies, customs and attitudes persist as obstacles to such families today ... so that we might together ease their burdens."

THREE

"Is this your room or do you share it with somebody else?" a teenaged boy asks 14-year-old Victoria Confino, as he surveys the 137-square-foot space. "I share it with a lot of somebody elses," she says. "I have five brothers."

The boy and his classmates have stepped back in time to 1916 to visit Victoria (played by an adult interpreter), who lived with her family at 97 Orchard Street. The often poignant details of daily life, as it was, are the soul of the Lower East Side Tenement Museum. Personal histories of actual residents explore universal themes and give the tours a sense of intimacy and emotional power. Each year, tens of thousands of visitors learn about these families, giving these otherwise untold sagas of hardship and hope a sense of historical permanence.

It took several years, however, before Abram found this home for those stories. In 1985, Abram and curator Anita Jacobson scoured the neighborhood for a suitable tenement to house a museum. It was a daunting task. Most early tenements had either been razed or renovated and those that remained weren't old enough to reflect the community's multi-ethnic history of German, Irish, Italian, Eastern European and Chinese immigrants, as well as formerly enslaved African-Americans. Abram and Jacobson eventually put their search aside and instead concentrated on developing public history programs that were, in effect, what Jacobson called "a museum without walls."

Then, in January 1988, while combing the neighborhood for office space, Jacobson spotted a "For Rent" sign at 97 Orchard Street. The storefront space of this five-story tenement was suitable and affordable.

left, The first floor hallway as it looked when the Tenement Museum moved into 97 Orchard Street in 1988.

below, During the initial restoration Museum staff discovered over 1,500 artifacts, including this calendar from the last year the building was occupied

bottom, A sign advertises a kitchen's use as a business.

When Jacobson asked where the bathrooms were, landlady Barbara Helpern led her through a dark hallway with a sheet metal ceiling, varnished burlap wallpaper and faded oil paintings. Helpern explaining that her family had owned the building since 1918, but that the 20 apartments had been vacant since 1935. In the apartments were furniture, crates of ginger ale and other items left untouched for half a century.

"It was as though people had just picked up and left," Jacobson recalled. "It was like a little time capsule. It was incredibly evocative. It was perfect for our needs."

The building, which is between Broome and Delancey Streets, is a pre-"Old Law" Tenement built in 1863 before the city had laws governing housing construction. At that time the cramped apartments lacked central heat, electricity and indoor plumbing. Through the years, the city passed new building codes and landlords made various modifications. The last round of laws, however, enacted during the Depression, prompted the Helperns to evict every family in their building rather than spend money to modernize. The laws didn't affect the tenement's commercial spaces and the four storefronts remained active.

In March 1988, the Museum moved in, working from the storefront but yearning to own the building. Amid a $3 million fund-raising campaign to purchase and restore 97 Orchard Street, the Museum opened on November 17, 1988, with an exhibit of Depression-era tenement photographs by Arnold Eagle, and a 50-seat storefront theater in which to host its programs. Over the next five years, the Museum featured an exhibit on the tragic 1911 Triangle Shirtwaist Factory fire, in which 146 garment workers died, and African-American and Chinese heritage walking tours.

Meanwhile, research began on the former residents, owners, and shopkeepers of 97 Orchard Street. Census material, court and voter records and countless other documents also shed light on the families, while a public search turned up former residents and descendants who supplied the museum with additional details. "If we were trying to be honest in the preservation of the tenement," Jacobson said, "then we should use the same approach with the people inside."

above, Most tenement dwellers had to provide their own stove. This one does double duty, c. 1936.

opposite, Advertising card for Professor Dora Meltzer the "unexcelled palmist", one of the more colorful businesses operating out of 97.

The front room of the Gumpertz apartment recreated to c. 1878.

Helping the Museum make that decision was a 1991 self-study funded by the National Endowment for the Humanities, which included research and discussions with museum professionals, poets, immigrant advocates, scholars and others. The study reinforced the decision to interpret the lives of real people and make the Museum's mission "promoting tolerance, as well as historical perspective."

National and international recognition soon followed, and in 1992, 97 Orchard Street joined estates like Mt. Vernon and Monticello on the National Register of Historic Places.

FOUR

The front room of the Gumpertz apartment at 97 Orchard Street looked as though a struggling seamstress had just stepped out for a break. Fabric swatches lay within reach of a Singer sewing machine, its foot pedal at rest, while clothes draped a dressing room screen. Just like in 1878.

In another tiny apartment, Adolpho Baldizzi's wooden tool chest sat on the linoleum floor while rosary beads belonging to his wife, Rosaria, hung from a mirror. Nearby, a photograph of President Franklin Delano Roosevelt adorned a wall. Just like in 1935.

It was neither 1878 nor 1935. It was October 3, 1994 and for the first time, visitors were invited into the tenement's newly restored apartments. "This is a pivotal moment in the history of museums," declared Abram, celebrating the debut of the museum's "Hard Time Stories and Morning Glories" tour. For the first time, an American house museum was honoring "the struggles, strategies, and triumphs of our urban, working-class immigrant forebears."

The Museum believed the Gumpertz and Baldizzi stories could provide comfort, inspiration and perspective to people coping with today's problems. Guests on this inaugural tour — later renamed "Getting By: Weathering the Great Depressions of 1873 and 1929" — learned how Natalie Gumpertz and Rosaria Baldizzi struggled in times of crisis, and who was there to help. Today's visitors can reflect on where they would turn at such times, and to consider those we might help today — and how.

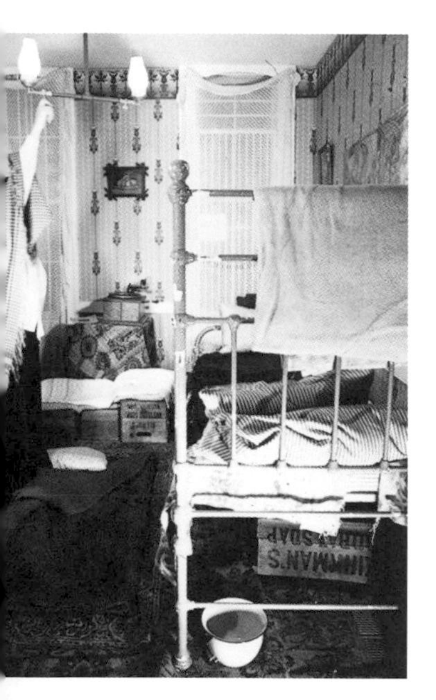

above, Sleeping arrangments for the Confino family apartment as conceived by the Museum.

opposite, The Baldizzi family kitchen c. 1935 as recreated at 97 Orchard.

Rich in history yet poor in pocket, the Museum was, in 1994, less than halfway to fulfilling its original $3 million capital campaign. And while the Museum managed to purchase 97 Orchard Street for $750,000 from the Helpern family in 1996, and completed its capital campaign one year later, financial pressures continued.

Despite these constraints, in 1997 the Museum debuted the Confino Family Apartment, its first hands-on, living history, family-oriented tour. Assuming the role of newcomers, children quizzed Victoria Confino (portrayed by a costumed interpreter) about everything from working in her father's factory to the chamber pots beneath her bed. For at least half the children who visit Victoria, the wrenching experience of immigration is real. Others struggle to understand the newcomers filling their classrooms and neighborhoods. These students barrage Victoria with questions about how she faced the many challenges they now endure — and learn they are not alone. This interactive program invites them to step into the shoes of an immigrant, building empathy for the experience of their foreign-born peers.

The Museum prepares each apartment in collaboration with leading historians and other experts. In 2001, an unusually diverse group was invited to view a mock-up of the 1897 home and dress factory of Harris and Jennie Levine. Packed in an intimate circle, leaders of traditionally adversarial sectors of today's garment industry — workers, contractors, retailers, unions — heard how this Russian Jewish immigrant family slept, ate, raised their children, and turned out hundreds of dresses in a dark 325-square-foot space that gave rise to the word "sweatshop." They then moved down the hall to visit the Rogarshevsky apartment as it looked in 1918: brightly lit, boasting major reforms the anti-sweatshop movement won for tenement families in the first decades of the 20th century. The Rogarshevsky home is seen when the family is mourning the loss of their patriarch, Abraham, a presser in a garment factory, to tuberculosis, a disease reformers hoped could be eradicated if garment work was

above, Today's garment workers struggle with hardships not that far removed from those of a century ago.

right, The recreated "dress factory" of Harris and Jennie Levine. The Levines turned out hundreds of dresses in a dark 325-square-foot space.

opposite, A participant in one of the Museum's immigrant programs.

removed from the home. At their visitors' suggestion, the Museum called the tour "Piecing It Together: Immigrants in the Garment Industry."

The experience helped these often clashing members of the garment industry begin a conversation among themselves on how to work together to combat the sweatshop phenomenon. They spent the rest of the day talking about a vision for the future.

Since then, the Museum has hosted dozens of public dialogues, with everyone from garment workers to immigrant youth turning to 97 Orchard Street's families for perspective.

Drawing connections between the stories of newcomers from every generation, the Museum established the first Immigrant Programs Department in any National Historic Site. New immigrants flock to the Museum for English classes that also explore how 97 Orchard Street's families faced the challenges of settling in America — and how they can do the same. "I not only learned English," said a recent graduate, "I learned I was not alone." When students said they lacked basic information about their rights and resources, the Museum responded by partnering with The New York Times on The New York Times Guide for Immigrants to New York City. Available in Spanish, Chinese and English, the Guide answers the most frequently asked questions and provides referrals to immigrant service organizations.

Ever-changing visual and digital art installations and theater programs give voice to the humor and ironies of immigrant life today. Far from a collection of static "period rooms," 97 Orchard Street has become the center of animated conversation about making it in — and remaking — America.

The next family to "move in" will be Joseph and Bridget Moore, an Irish Catholic waiter and his wife who lived at 97 Orchard in 1869, in the aftermath of the Civil War and the bloody New York City draft riots. The first permanent exhibit of Irish working-class life in a National Historic Site, the Moore home will explore a time and a people who inspired fundamental questions with which we still grapple: Who is American? What does it mean to be a citizen?

These powerful stories of immigrant lives have brought a flood of visitors to the Museum. Between 1999 and 2001, attendance doubled. Visitors came from every state in the union, as well as 33 countries. Now, over 105,000 visitors come annually, more than to many of the largest history museums in the city. In the effort to make the museum accessible to all, the Museum offers touch tours, American Sign Language tours, and tours in Spanish, Chinese, Russian and other languages.

In 1998, the National Trust for Historic Preservation designated the Museum's tenement an affiliated site. The same year, the Museum became an affiliate of the National Park Service, linking it with the immigrant landmarks at Ellis Island, Castle Clinton and the Statue of Liberty.

As a National Endowment for the Humanities panel observed, "The Tenement Museum is a benchmark institution — the whole museum community waits to see what they are doing next to set the standard." The Museum works to establish a new role for historic sites in civic life, in its own neighborhood and around the world. Through the Lower East Side Community Preservation Project, it collaborates with community leaders to identify and interpret Lower East Side histories, and uses them to inspire dialogue about community issues. The Museum organized the International Coalition of Historic Site Museums of Conscience, including the District Six Museum in South Africa and the Gulag Museum in Russia, to help sites the world over inspire visitors to become actively engaged in issues from slavery to poverty.

Most important, the Museum continues daily to educate, entertain and inspire. In the Baldizzi apartment, Josephine Esposito's recording can be heard describing her childhood at 97 Orchard Street. When she tells how her mother overstarched her blouses with Linit and scrubbed Josephine clean in the kitchen sink, visitors nod their heads or smile in recognition. Some are moved to tears. Even if their families never lived on the Lower East Side, they discover similarities between their experiences and Esposito's, and they feel connected to all the lives lived in this tenement.

Their reaction to Esposito's stories is the ultimate validation of the journey her father made as a stowaway from Palermo to the Lower East Side. "I'm so proud for my parents," Josephine said. "I wish they were here to see all this."

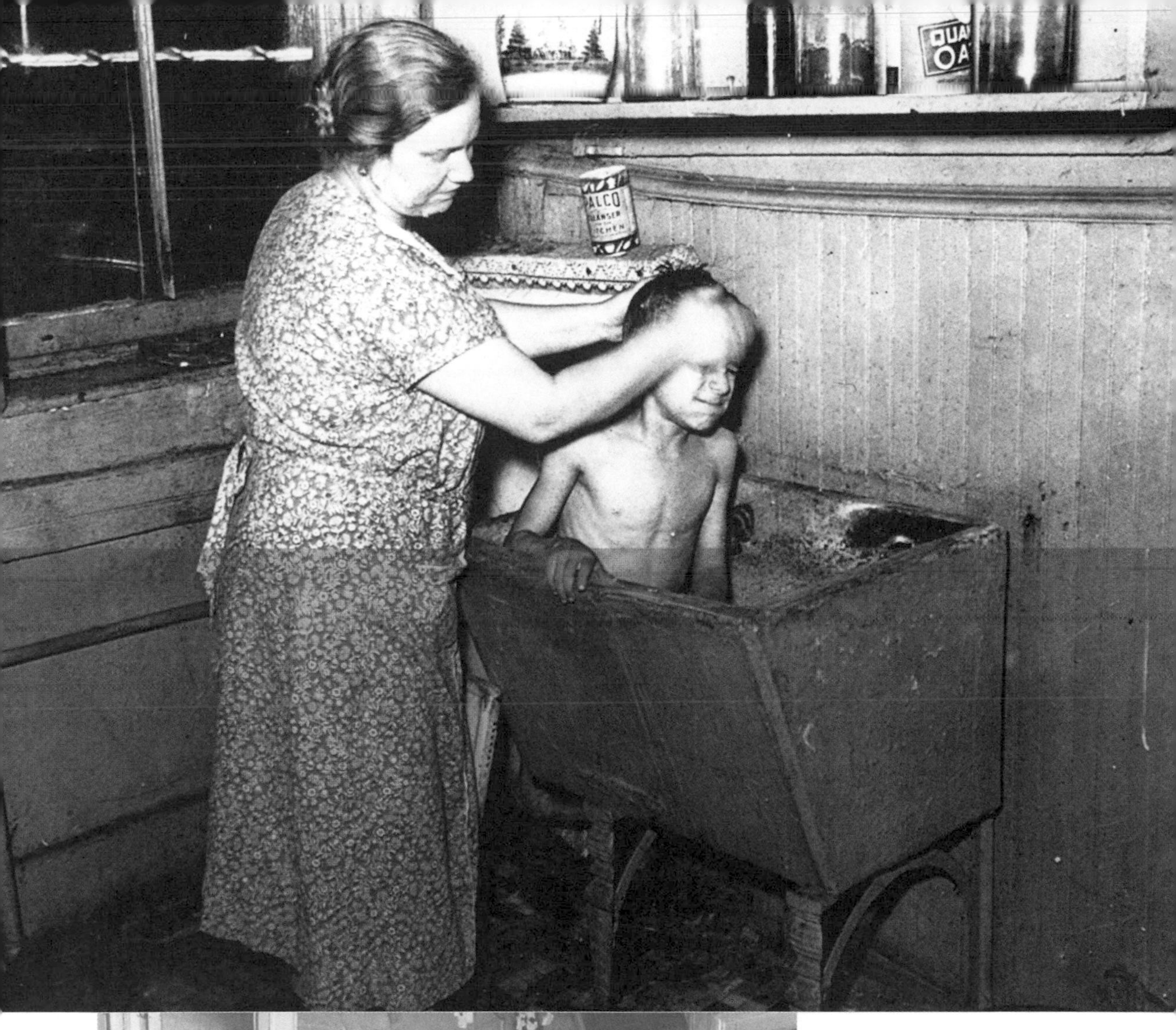

above, Children were often bathed in the tenement kitchen's slop sink.

left, A tenement kitchen at 97 Orchard.

97 Orchard Street
E. 13th
E. 12th
E. 11th
E. 10th
E. 9th
E. 8th ST.
E. 7th
E. 6th
E. 5th
E. 4th
E. 3rd
E. 2nd
E. 1st
TOMPKINS SQUARE
DRY DOCK ST.
BROADWAY
WANAMAKER PL.
STUYVESANT ST.
ST. MARK'S
ASTOR
COOPER SQ.
FOURTH
THIRD
SECOND
FIRST
AVENUE
BOWERY
GREAT JONES ST.
BOND ST.
BLEECKER
HOUSTON
LAFAYETTE
STANTON
RIVINGTON
SCHIFF PKWY.
DELANCEY
KENMARE
BROOME
GRAND
HOWARD
HESTER
CANAL
WALKER
WHITE
FRANKLIN
LEONARD
WORTH
PEARL
DUANE
CHAMBERS
CITY HALL PARK
ROOSEVELT PARK
DELANCEY
SARAH
CHRYSTIE
FORSYTH
ELDRIDGE
ALLEN
ORCHARD
LUDLOW
ESSEX
NORFOLK
SUFFOLK
CLINTON
ATTORNEY
RIDGE
PITT
WILLETT
SHERIFF
COLUMBIA
CANNON
LEWIS
GOERCK
MANGIN
HAMILTON FISH PARK
SEWARD PARK
JEFFERSON
RUTGERS
MONTGOMERY
GOUVERNEUR
SCAMMEL
JACKSON
CHERRY
WATER
CORLEARS HOOK PARK
PIKE
DIVISION
EAST BROADWAY
HENRY
MARKET
MONROE
MADISON
CATHARINE
OLIVER
JAMES
CHATHAM SQ.
BAYARD
MULBERRY
MOTT
ELIZABETH
BAXTER
CENTRE
PELL ST.
DOYERS
PARK
FOLEY SQ.
NEW CHAMBERS
WILLIAM
ROSE
VANDEWATER
NEW BOWERY
OAK
SOUTH
FRANKFORT
SPRUCE
BEEKMAN
FERRY
DOVER
PECK SLIP
MANHATTAN BRIDGE
BROOKLYN BRIDGE
EAST RIVER

PART II THE LOWER EAST SIDE

The East Village. Kleindeutschland. Loisaida. Five Points. Chinatown. Little Italy. The Bowery. The Jewish Quarter. Alphabet City.

The Lower East Side has been named and renamed countless times as every generation of newcomers marked its own turf. This four-square-mile tract, from 14th Street south to Fulton Street, from Broadway and Pearl Street to the East River, has always been a protean neighborhood that defies a tidy summary.

During the nineteenth century, the Lower East Side included both the city's most notorious slum — the five Points, near present-day Columbus Park — and upscale areas like Colonnade Row near Astor Place, home to financier John Jacob Astor and writer Washington Irving.

James DeLancey, Britain's Lieutenant Governor of New York

In the 1600s, Dutch colonists divided the homeland of Native Americans into eight farms; in the next century, under British rule, these farms were consolidated into larger tracts. James DeLancey, Britain's Lieutenant Governor of New York, bought approximately 300 acres (120 city blocks), mostly north of Division Street. After DeLancey died in 1760, his family remained loyal to Britain, even retreating to England during the American Revolution. After the war, the DeLancey tract was confiscated and sold off in lots the size of city blocks, much of it to merchants and lawyers. In fact, all Tory property in New York was forfeited, marking a turning point in the history of Manhattan real estate as the city redistributed among the middle- and

"Against the [walls] are hung unused hats of odd colors and still odder shapes, musical instruments of various kinds, pots, kettles, pans, pokers, joints of raw meat... strings of Bologna sausages, the gowns of women and great pipes.... None of the chairs have backs and [few] have four legs"

James D. McCabe, on a typical Mulberry Street home, *New York by Sunlight and Gaslight*, 1882

upper middle-classes huge chunks of land once belonging to wealthy Loyalists.

By the early nineteenth century, the Lower East Side had evolved into the city's manufacturing center, while shipyards and slaughterhouses lined the neighborhood's waterfront. Before cars and subways, workers lived close to their jobs, filling the neighborhood with working poor, including Irish immigrants and free blacks who in 1820 each comprised 20 percent of the local population. Most resided in the Five Points slum, while nearby Catherine Street boasted fledgling shops like Lord & Taylor and Brooks Brothers.

above, A Baxter Street tenement shown in cut-away, 1880s

opposite, The Five Points depicted in the 1850s

In 1833, a builder sensing a market for small, cheap, multi-family homes erected what many historians believe to be the first tenement in New York City on Water Street near Corlear's Hook. Others soon followed. These buildings often replaced old, single-family frame houses or row houses that had been sub-divided into ad-hoc multiple units. Tenements were a quick, cheap solution to housing the tens of thousands of immigrants who poured into the Lower East Side during the mid-nineteenth century.

The city's population doubled between 1845 and 1860, with the Lower East Side absorbing Irish immigrants escaping the Famine and Germans fleeing civil strife, as well as Puerto Rican and Cuban intellectuals and cigar makers plotting independence from Spain. While Irish and Caribbean immigrants settled throughout the city, but especially the southern half of the Lower East Side, Germans clustered together north of Division Street. The area became known as Kleindeutschland, or Little Germany, with Avenue B referred to as "German Broadway." These immigrants — mostly Catholic Bavarians — worked as tailors, shoemakers, cabinetmakers, upholsterers and in other skilled professions, and even helped start the trade union movement. In 1871, Kleindeutschland was the equivalent of the fifth-largest German city in the world. (By the 1880s, many Bavarians had moved from the neighborhood, replaced increasingly by Protestant and Jewish Prussians.)

Virtually all of these immigrants lived in tenements, where "the greatest amount of profit is sought to be realized from the least amount of space, with little or no regard for the health, comfort, or protection of the lives of the tenants," declared the Superintendent of Buildings in 1862. At this time, tenement construction was not subject to regulation.

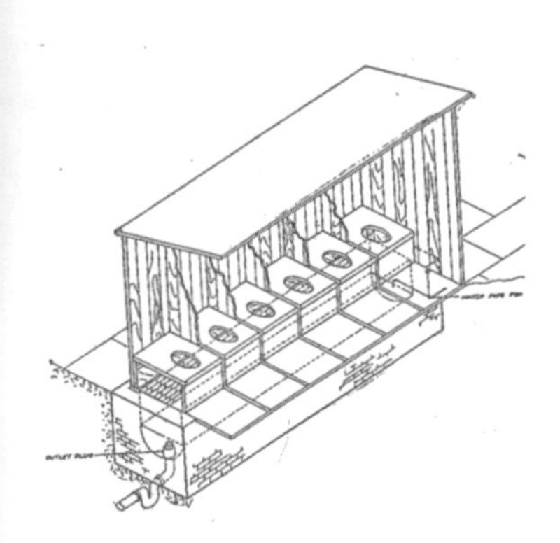

above, A diagram of a tenement's "school sink" outhouse.

opposite, Tenement backyards c. 1895. Note school sinks on the lower right.

In 1867 — four years after 97 Orchard Street was built — the state passed the first housing reform and defined tenements as any building that was rented to three or more unrelated families. Tenements signified a new form of coexistence — and a new set of conflicts. As a "civilized society," what were the minimum health and safety standards New York should provide? And who was responsible for providing them? The Tenement House Law required, among other things; that new tenements be equipped with one outside privy for every 20 occupants. Between 1866 and 1873, 34 tenements were built on a five-block stretch of Orchard Street.

Then, in 1879, another round of regulations ("Old Law") mandated that new tenements consume no more than 65 percent of a 25-by-100-foot lot (allowing for larger

“That several hundred thousand people in the city have no proper facilities for keeping their bodies clean is a disgrace to the city and to the civilization of the nineteenth century.”

The New York Times January 18, 1895

In 1903 the square block on which sits the Lower East Side Tenement Museum was the most crowded block in the most densely-populated place on earth.

backyards), and that apartments be better ventilated, with windows that opened onto a narrow air shaft. The shape of their revised floor plans led them to be dubbed "dumbbell tenements." The Board of Health, however, had limited enforcement power and the laws were largely flouted.

Nonetheless, even the worst of these dingy, unhealthy and unsafe tenements attracted tenants as the Lower East Side was inundated with an unprecedented crush of newcomers from 1880 to 1924. Many were Italians, joined by massive numbers of Jewish immigrants. From 1880 to 1890 alone, 60,000 Jews from Eastern Europe settled on the Lower East Side. In the 1910s they were joined by Sephardic Jews from Greece, Syria and other parts of the former Ottoman Empire. And even in the face of the first law to bar immigrants from entering the country based solely on race — the 1882 Chinese Exclusion Act — New York's Chinese population nearly tripled between 1890 and 1900, with migrants from California and other Western states.

The 10th Ward, stretching from Rivington to Division Streets and from the Bowery to Norfolk Street, was said to be the most densely populated place on earth. The Tenement Commission reported in 1903 that the square block that became home to the Lower East Side Tenement Museum had over 2,000 residents, making it the most crowded block in the most crowded neighborhood in the world.

Lower East Side peddlers on Hester Street, c. 1898.

These immigrants would change the face of America forever, joining middle class reformers in fighting for better places to live. The exposés of social activists like Jacob Riis and Lillian Wald paved the way for the Tenement House Law of 1901 (or "New Law"), which banned new dumbbell tenements and mandated change in extant tenements.

Landlords had to improve hallway lighting and construct one indoor toilet for every two families. The law also established the Tenement House Department to enforce the statute.

Outside the tenements, the streets resounded with the cacophony of peddlers hawking their wares from pushcarts. They grew ever more crowded as the neighborhood's population peaked at 550,000 in 1910. Old-stock Gothamites continued to disdain this flood of immigrants, as they had earlier newcomers.

Eventually, these nativists had their way. In the 1920s, Congress passed a series of restrictive quotas. Social reformers finally succeeded in having thousands of tenements razed to widen streets and build parks; other tenements gave way for the approaches to the Williamsburg and Manhattan Bridges. Combined, these changes reduced by half the population of the Lower East Side, and left vacant thousands of apartments.

A 1934 amendment to the Multiple Dwellings Law mandated expensive alterations, including fire-proofing the public hallways in existing tenements. Rather than make costly improvements, many landlords — including the owner of 97 Orchard Street — financially strapped because of the Depression, evicted their tenants and closed their buildings. Later, Mayor Fiorello H. LaGuardia demolished thousands of tenements and offered a new solution for housing the poor — the public housing project.

A tenement family, c. 1905.

"To the cry of ... 'Abolish the tenements!'.... Why not abolish the tenants?"

John Van Dyke, *The New New York* 1909

above, A drawing of "First Houses," the first public housing project in the United States.

opposite, A vibrant Puerto Rican community took hold in the 1960s, and the area above Houston Street became known as Loisaida.

In 1934, the nation's first locally constructed public housing project, First Houses, arose on Third Street and Avenue A. Though the doors of America were still locked to many, after World War II the neighborhood was transformed again by internal migration. African-Americans from the South joined descendants of some of the first residents of the Lower East Side, and Puerto Ricans — U.S. citizens since 1917 — flocked to the neighborhood to fill some of the city's last remaining manufacturing jobs. Over the next two decades, Puerto Rican activists built home town clubs and crowned the area north of Houston Street as Loisaida. Artists and musicians from around the country established a new bohemia.

Puerto Rican activists built home town clubs and crowned the area north of Houston Street as Loisaida.

TEL:(212)614-9948 Cel:917-968-3618
ELECTRONICS
& CAMERA
110-220 VOLTS
מוצרי חשמל לארץ
ISRAEL GIFT
DEPT.
17
APARTMENTS
FOR RENT
(212)
475-6660

Immigrants from 36 nations and four generations collaborate, clash and create new cultures every day. It is this creative tension that has made the Lower East Side a dynamic incubator of change.

As part of the legal victories of the civil rights movement, nation-based quotas were finally abolished in 1965. Thousands of immigrants from East Asia redefined a decaying Chinatown; soon the neighborhood boasted communities speaking at least five Chinese dialects.

above, In the 1970s and 80s many square blocks of Lower East Side tenements were abandoned and destroyed.

opposite, Essex Street today

But in the 1960s and 1970s, the manufacturing jobs that had been the lifeblood of immigrants for more than a century all but vanished. People fled. Between 1974 and 1979, the area north of Houston Street lost two-thirds of its population. But real estate speculators saw the opportunity to buy property cheap and develop new housing.

By the end of the 1990s, the neighborhood south of Houston Street had been transformed. In 1997, a one-bedroom co-op on Grand Street cost $50,000. Today, they fetch over $250,000. Many residents welcomed the new cafes, fashion boutiques and safer streets over the painful years of violence and decay. But as a 1998 New York Times article noted, "What some people view as a renaissance others see as displacement of the poor."

Today, new arrivals toil in sweatshops above chic boutiques; botánicas flank trendy bars; and immigrants from 36 nations and four generations collaborate, clash and create new cultures every day. This is the creative tension that has made the Lower East Side a dynamic incubator of change for nearly 200 years.

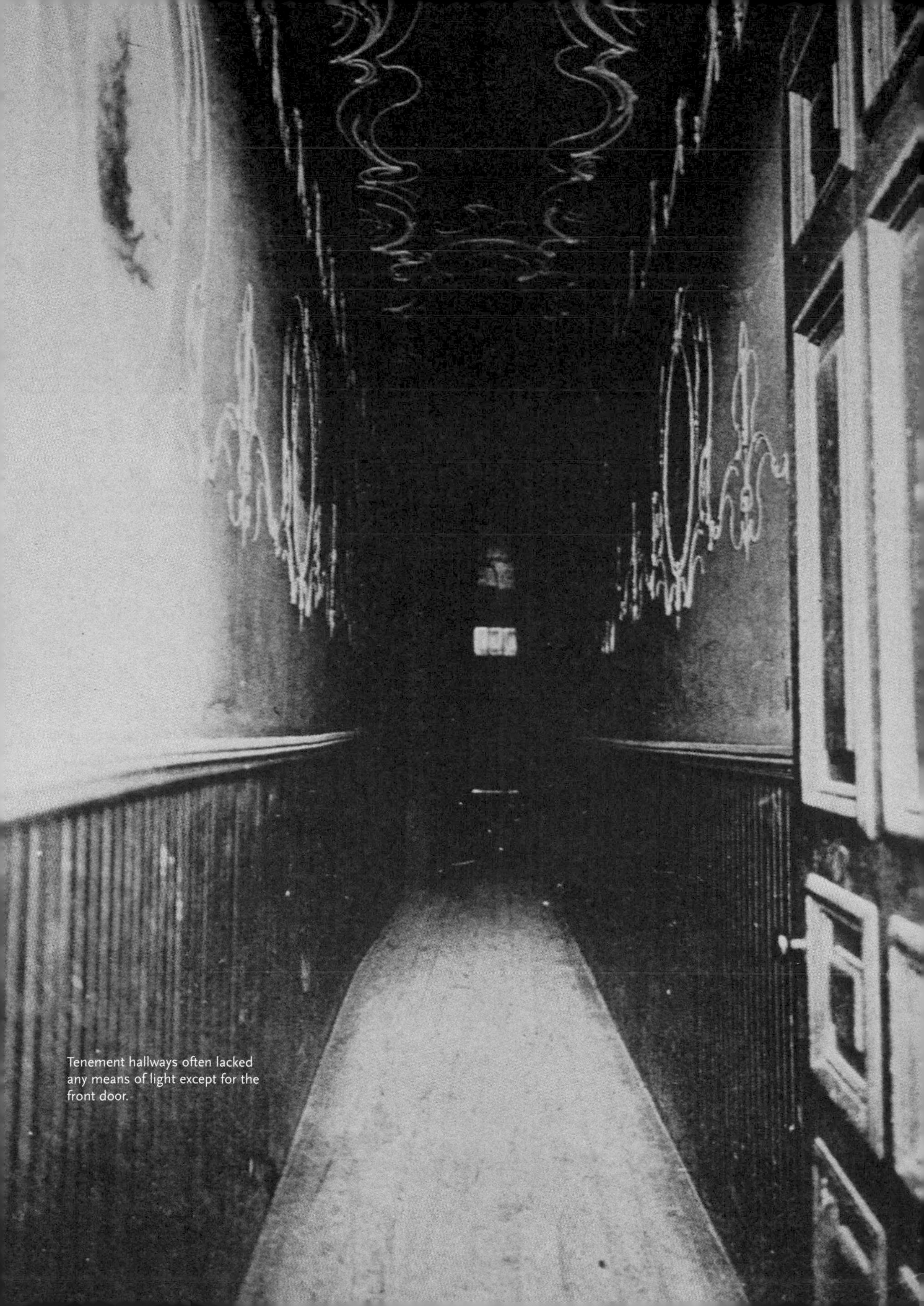

Tenement hallways often lacked any means of light except for the front door.

PART III 97 ORCHARD STREET

ONE

On a winter's day in 1863, Lucas Glockner, a German-born tailor, tried to divine the future in a small parcel of land on Orchard Street. Glockner had been in America 20 years, and in those two decades, millions of Irish immigrants and his fellow Germans had landed on these shores. Living on the Lower East Side, Glockner had no doubt witnessed the neighborhood's rapid growth. Landowners were building multi-family tenements to accommodate the surging population and to replace the old, often haphazardly divided, single-family homes. At age 42, Glockner was now a landowner himself with plans to erect a building that would provide both a home for himself and his Bavarian-born wife, Wilhemena, and a small measure of prosperity. Most tenements earned landlords about a 20 percent return on their investments.

Glockner's plot of land had changed hands many times in the two centuries before he bought it. In the 1640s, the property was a small part of a larger farm owned by the Dutch West India Company. In the 1700s, James DeLancey had a fruit orchard at his farm's northern edge and the dirt road leading there was subsequently named Orchard Street. Some time before 1811, when the whole of Manhattan was mapped out in a grid of standard 25-by-100-foot lots, the

THE GLOCKNERS

BUILDER/LANDLORD OF 97 ORCHARD

The tenement at 97 Orchard Street brought owner Lucas Glockner and his wife Wilhelmina the prosperity of which they had always dreamed. The 1870 census listed Glockner's personal wealth at $1,800 (two to three times more than most families in the building). His real estate, which by that point included several other properties, was valued at an impressive $45,000. In fact, by 1870, the Glockners and their children—Oscar, 11, William, 5, and Arthur, 1—had moved into a presumably larger, more modern home at 25 Allen Street. The couple's two daughters Minnie and Ida, were born there between 1871 and 1877.

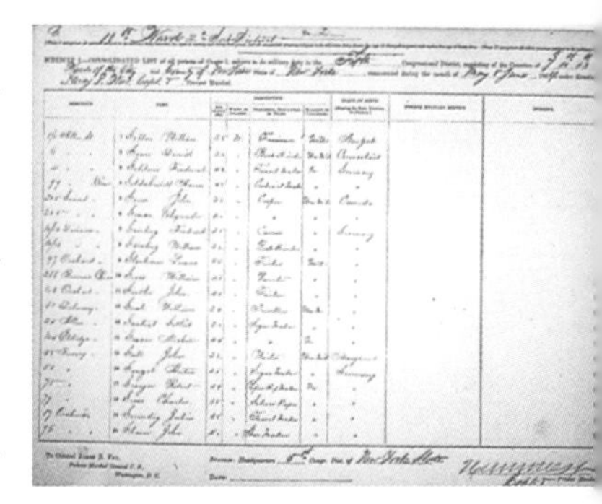

above, Lucas Glockner's draft record, indicating he registered for the Civil War in 1864.

One Glockner remained at 97 Orchard Street: Lucas' eldest son, Edward, a 24-year-old bookbinder. His wife, Caroline Stockel, 22, was an immigrant from Saxony and her parents, Louisa and August also lived in the building. The Glockners were financially secure (Edward had a personal wealth of $600), but the family was not immune from tragedy and their six-month-old daughter, Louisa, died of bronchitis in March 1870.

After Lucas Glockner left 97, he proved a stable landlord, keeping the building for 23 years until 1886. He sold it to a man named William Morris, who then sold it two months later; the building proceeded to change hands 13 times between 1886 and 1907. Like Glockner, all the subsequent owners were immigrants.

By the time Glockner died of a cerebral hemorrhage in 1891, two weeks shy of his 71st birthday, he was living nearby at 152 Henry Street. His two eldest sons had by then migrated to East Harlem and Newark, New Jersey.

plot where the Museum now stands was carved into a 25-by-89-foot space. In 1814, John Jacob Astor bought four adjoining lots, including the future site of 97 Orchard Street. A German immigrant, Astor arrived in New York at 21 and rapidly earned a fortune as a furrier and financier. Around 1810, he began investing heavily in Manhattan real estate, ultimately becoming the largest landowner in the city. Astor was an investor not a developer, and in 1827, he sold three empty lots on Orchard Street to the Dutch Reformed Protestant Church. The congregation built the lots' first structure, the Orchard Street Church.

In 1862, Glockner and two other tailors from Germany, Jacob Walter, and Adam Stumm had purchased the three adjoining Orchard Street lots from the Second Reformed Presbyterian Church, which had taken over the tract in 1860. On February 28, 1863, Glockner and his partners divvied up the property, with Glockner taking the middle lot. Next door at 99 Orchard Street, Adam Stumm built an identical five-story tenement — a simple brick Italianate structure with cornice topping, steep stone stoop and 20 apartments with two basement level commercial shops.

Lucas Glockner's tenement was originally a welcome alternative to the rapidly deteriorating row houses converted into ad hoc multi-family dwellings. Glockner took such pride in 97 Orchard Street that he moved his family there from St. Mark's Place.

The Moores' daughter Jane in her later years, with her husband.

THE MOORES

Bridget Meehan was just seventeen when she made the long journey from Ireland to New York City in 1863. Thousands of young women like her braved immigration alone, escaping poverty to find work as domestics in well-to-do Protestant households. Joseph Peter Moore, the man who would become her husband, arrived two years later and found work as a waiter and a bartender. As Joseph and Bridget were growing up, nearly a third of their fellow Irish disappeared: over 1 million died, and another 1.5 million left the country.

But Joseph and Bridget's migrations didn't end once they arrived in America. Almost every year, they moved to a different apartment in the Lower East Side, as their fortunes fell, rose, and fell again. They came to 97 Orchard Street in 1869 as one of the few Irish families in Kleindeutschland, or Little Germany.

As a bartender, Joseph would have stood at the center of an immigrant revolution in New York politics. Under the direction of the infamous Tammany, the saloon was the immi grant Lower East Side's town hall – where votes were cast (and recast), citizenship papers were drawn, and power was built.

Bridget spent most of her life in New York either pregnant or nursing. But of 11 children she bore, nine perished. After crossing the ocean to escape famine, Bridget saw some of her children die of diseases related to malnutrition or contaminated food. While at 97 Orchard Street, the Moores lost ten-month-old Agnes Mary Moore to marasmus. Bridget died in childbirth at the age of 36, leaving Joseph to carry on with his two surviving daughters, Mary and Jane.

THE GUMPERTZES

Nathalie Gumpertz
c. 1880.

below,
The bedroom in the
Gumpertz apartment.

Julius Gumpertz and Nathalie Rheinsberg both Prussian immigrants, met and married in New York. Both were Jewish and around 22 when they emigrated, and likely left home for economic opportunity not religious freedom.

By 1870, the couple had settled at 97. Julius was a shoemaker, a trade he may have learned in Europe. But in America, the industry was in decline and Julius soon moved on, becoming a small-time merchant. An economic depression in 1873 (nearly a quarter of New York's labor force lost their jobs) eventually forced Julius back into the shoe trade, where he worked as a heel cutter.

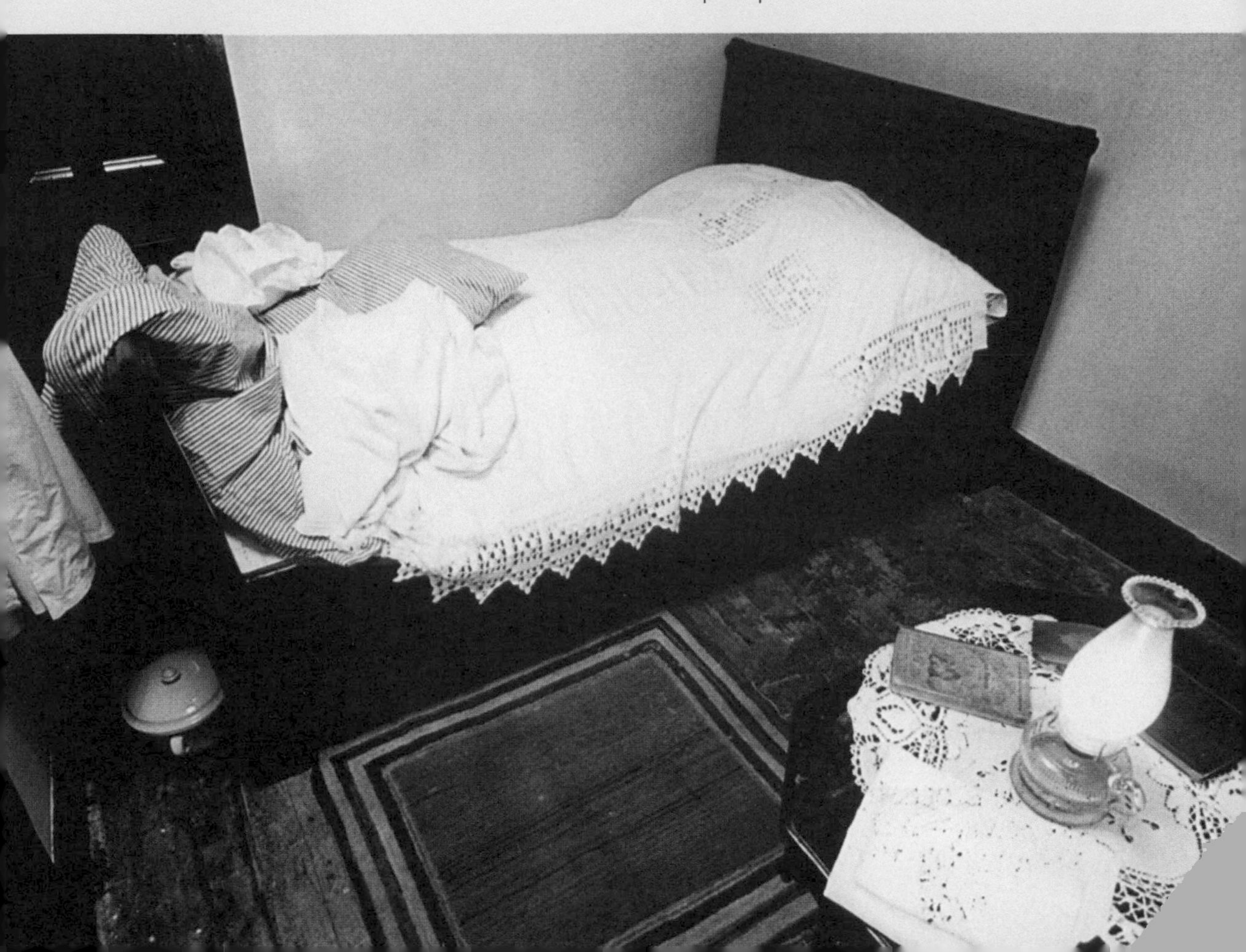

TWO

It is fitting that a museum celebrating the histories of ordinary people is housed in a building that is far from unique architecturally. The tenement at 97 Orchard Street represents the experience of home shared by millions of immigrants in New York. Each three-room flat was a mere 325 square feet. The front room served many functions: During the day a tenant might sew there to earn a living; in the evening it became the dining room and then the parlor; finally at night, it was converted into a bedroom. The middle room was the kitchen. If the tenants owned a coal-burning stove, it was their only source of heat. Next came the main bedroom, a cramped affair at only 67 square feet. This windowless interior room — like the kitchen — was extremely stuffy and dark.

Today, we might not appreciate how much light — natural and artificial — brightens our homes. In the early days, the building's narrow hallways were virtually pitch black. Gas lights weren't installed until the 1890s. And inside the apartments, only the front rooms had two windows and the light they admitted was often blocked by nearby tenements. But in the 1860s and 1870s, this was widely accepted as an improvement over the decrepit, wooden one-family homes that had been subdivided and subdivided again to accommodate multiple families.

As the neighborhood's population exploded, with more and more immigrants packed in to buildings like 97

On October 7, 1874 Julius Gumpertz left home at 7 a.m. for work in lower Manhattan. Nathalie stayed home with their four young children, Rosa, Nannie, Olga and Isaac, who ranged from age seven to eleven months. By day's end, Julius had vanished without a trace. It is speculated that perhaps the tough economic times prompted Julius' departure for it was not uncommon for husbands to desert their families.

Eight months after Julius disappeared, their son Isaac died from dysentery. Although most married women didn't work in 1874, Nathalie needed a means of support immediately. She chose the most common path available to women and became one of New York City's 35,000 dressmakers and milliners, converting her front room into a workshop.

Nathalie probably charged around ten dollars to make a new dress and five dollars to update an old one. Each order could take up to five fittings. Neighborhood women typically provided fabrics, notions and fashion illustrations depicting the style they wanted as their own. For this demanding work, Nathalie earned about $7.50 a week, enough to pay the rent and keep her children in school, although her daughters probably helped baste, sew and serve waiting customers coffee and cake in the kitchen.

Nine years after Julius' departure, his father died in Germany, leaving a $600 inheritance. Nathalie went to court to have her husband declared legally dead. Lucas Glockner and John Schneider testified about what Schneider called Julius' "sudden, mysterious and unexplained disappearance... and the diligent and unsuccessful search for him." Nathalie was awarded the money and left the increasingly Eastern European Lower East Side for Yorkville, a relatively suburban German community on the Upper East Side. She remained in Yorkville until 1894 when she died of a cerebral hemorrhage at age 58.

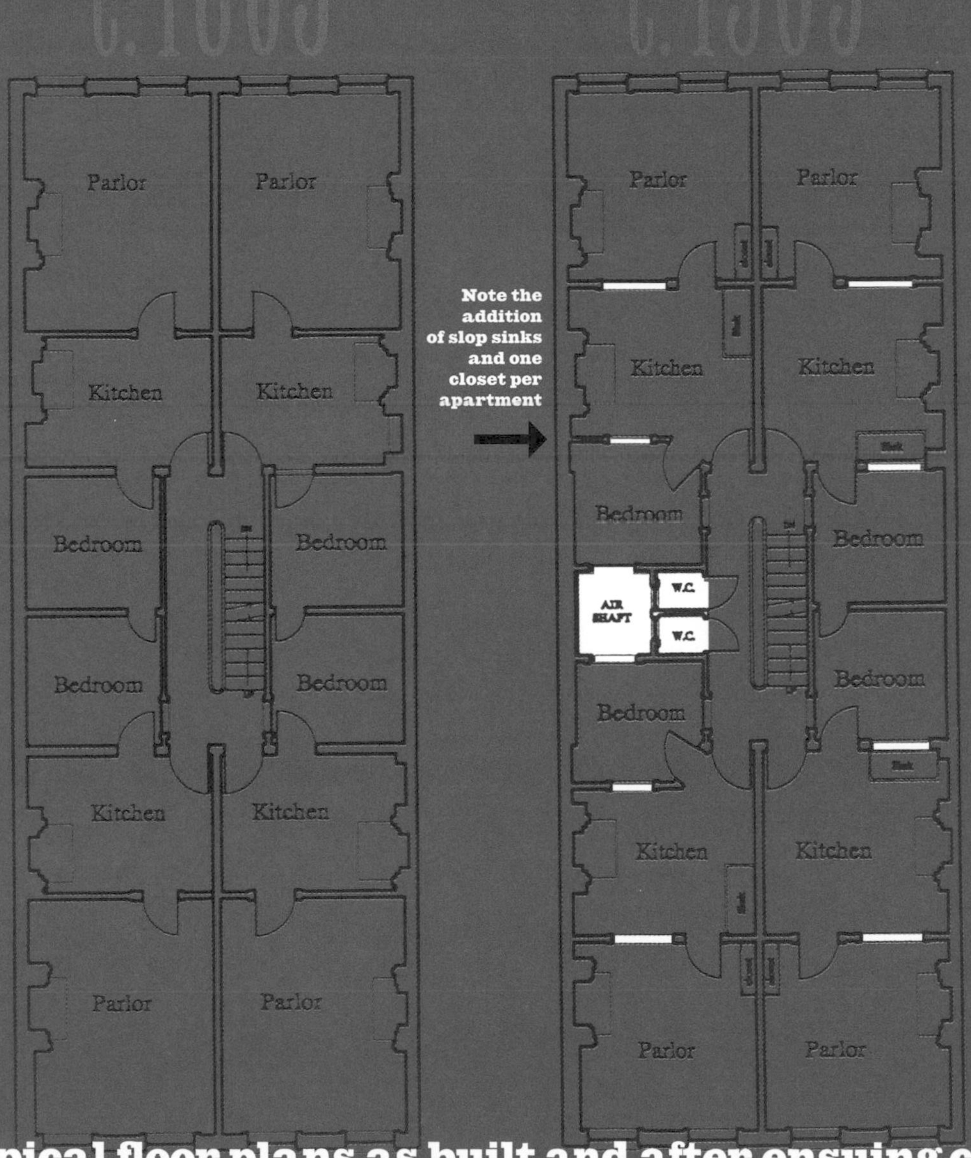

Typical floor plans as built and after ensuing code improvements. Major alterations included the addition of an airshaft, two hallway toilets per floor, and interior windows cut through for light.

Jennie and Harris Levine, 1924.

Orchard Street, concerns about disease, hygiene, crime and even morality fueled a movement to make air and light a human right.

The Tenement House Act of 1901 required, among other things, that light and ventilation be substantially improved in hallways and apartments. Translucent glass panels were cut into wooden apartment doors and windows were carved into walls separating rooms, exposing interior rooms to light and air filtering through the front room's windows. A ventilating skylight with a glazed surface was installed over the stairway and gas lights were required to burn in hallways from sunset to 10 p.m. Edison had installed electric street lamps downtown in 1882, but it wasn't until the 1920s that electricity was installed at 97 Orchard Street.

During the building's early years, 97 Orchard Street had no indoor plumbing, even though many other city buildings did. After drawing water from a hand pump in the backyard, residents had to haul heavy buckets up to their apartments. It likely took several trips simply to fill a basin or sink. Indoor running water was installed after the city's health department won the right — in an 1895 court ruling — to mandate plumbing.

The hand pump was not the only utilitarian feature of the back yard. These small outdoor areas were places to wash and hang laundry and to answer nature's call. When the Museum's team of urban archaeologists researched the

THE LEVINES

According to family lore, in 1890 newlyweds Harris and Jennie Levine came to New York on their honeymoon from Plonsk, in what's now Poland. Within two years, they set up a dressmaking shop in their parlor, joining the 100 other immigrant-run shops on Orchard Street, in the heart of America's clothing capital.

The Levines recruited three others to help them – two young women, to do the basting and the finishing, and one man to wield the heavy irons that pressed the fabric. Harris crouched over the sewing machine by the dim light of the window, while Jennie cared for the extended "family" that made up the Levine's shop: cooking stew for the workers, boiling diapers for her two-year-old son Hyman. In November of 1897, Jennie gave birth to her third child, Max, in a tiny bedroom just a few feet from the presser's station.

Harris faced fierce competition: on his block alone, 23 other contractors raced to produce more, cheaper, faster. This drove down to miserable levels what Harris, and in turn, his workers, could expect to make for each piece. Despite a law prohibiting more than 60 hours of work a week, many workers toiled from dawn to dusk to make ends meet.

After nearly ten years in the same three rooms, in 1905 the Levines moved to Brooklyn. They followed hundreds of other tenement-shop owners moving to larger loft factories uptown and in the outer boroughs – factories that would mark the next era in clothing manufacture, politics, and immigrant working life.

Morris Rogarshevsky in 1921.
He later changed the family name to Rosenthal.

Fannie on the roof of 97, c.1920.

THE ROGARSHEVSKYS

Although 97 Orchard Street experienced astonishing turnover, one family stands as an exception. Others eagerly moved on, but this Orthodox Jewish family stayed for over a quarter of a century, leaving only after all the building's residents were evicted.

Abram and Zipe Heller and their five children emigrated from Telz, Lithuania in 1901, adopting the name of their American sponsor, Rogarshevsky, and Americanizing their first names to Abraham and Fannie. Their infant daughter, Heinde, soon died of diptheria, but two sons, Henry and Philip, were born in the next few years. Sometime between 1906 and 1910, this family of eight moved from a nearby tenement to 97 Orchard Street, as did Fannie's parents, the Bayards.

In an oral history, Henry recalled how he and his three brothers slept on a couch in the front room, while his two sisters shared a folding cot. In summer, the family often slept on the fire escape or roof. Abraham, who was a leader of a local synagogue, toiled as a presser in a garment shop. By 1910, his three eldest children also worked—Ida, 18, and Bessie, 16, in the garment industry and Morris, 14, as a shipping clerk.

During the next few years, Ida and Bessie married and moved out. To make ends meet, the family took in a boarder, Clara Kaplan, a 48-year-old Russian immigrant. Morris, who was working as a furrier, soon married and moved out. Another son, Samuel, who was among other things, an aspiring boxer who nicknamed himself Rocky, an undertaker and a taxi driver, married and remained at 97 Orchard Street.

Abraham Rogarshevsky, c. 1915.

In 1918, the patriarch, Abraham took ill with tuberculosis, a grave but common disease. Abraham's *lands-man-schaft* (an organization of people from the same home town) would have paid for the occasional doctor's visit, but mostly the family would have used home remedies like "cupping." After rubbing a glass cup with alcohol, a flame was held under the cup to burn out the oxygen. The cup was then pressed to the chest or back, supposedly drawing consumption from the lungs. Their efforts, however, could not check the disease and Abraham died on July 12.

Fannie, who was unemployed and spoke no English, found a sympathetic landlord in Moishe Helpern. Helpern had fled Russian pogroms and established himself as a peddler in New York. He made Fannie the building's janitor, allowing her to live rent-free in exchange for her work.

At the same time Morris Rogarshevsky's wife died and Morris, also suffering from consumption, moved back home to 97 Orchard Street. Under Fannie's watchful eye, Morris recovered, and later remarried. In 1925 he opened his own furrier business and changed the family's name to Rosenthal.

Ten years later, when the residents of 97 Orchard Street were evicted, Fannie Rosenthal stayed on as the janitor and later moved with her son Phillip and daughter-in-law Miriam into the Vladeck Houses, one of the country's first public housing projects, near the Williamsburg Bridge.

tenement's early toilet facilities, they expected to find an old-fashioned outhouse, a deep and odiferous privy pit cleaned only periodically. Instead, they unearthed evidence suggesting that early residents had used a water-cleansed brick vault connected to a sewage system, a more sanitary and modern facility than standard outhouses found in other nineteenth-century yards. In 1864, the Council on Hygiene and Public Health reported that the ward in which 97 Orchard Street is located had complete sewerage; the area was one of the most "salubrious" in the city. As primitive as these early methods were, they suggest a more healthful existence than the general stereotype of early tenement living.

To comply with the 1901 Tenement House Act, the landlord installed one indoor toilet for every two families, or two per floor. Families, however, held onto their chamber pots as one toilet could be shared by more than a dozen people.

In fact, the new law preceded a major facelift at 97 Orchard Street. In 1905, the first-floor front apartments were converted into storefronts, and cast-iron stairs replaced the stone stoop. The landlord also spruced up the front hall, adding a tile floor, pressed sheet metal ceilings, oil paintings and a burlap wall covering varnished with shellac. The hallway's medallion-style pastoral paintings remain a mystery and it's uncertain whether they were an artist's creation or standard paint-by-numbers decoration.

The Confino family, c. 1914, shortly after their arrival in the U.S.

THE CONFINOS

Abraham and Rachel Confino were a well-educated, Sephardic Jewish couple with a well-appointed house, servants, gardens and vineyards in Kastoria, Turkey. But around 1913 outside forces pushed the family down the immigrant path toward the tenements of the Lower East Side.First, the couple's eldest daughter, 16-year-old Allegra was steered into an arranged marriage with Sam Russo, a Kastorian native. She reluctantly accompanied him to the Lower East Side. Her younger brother Joe also left for New York, perhaps fearing conscription into the Greek army. (Troops had been quartered in the Confino home, and Kastoria eventually fell to Greece.) Worst of all, a fire annihilated the Confino's house and Abraham's grocery. Wiped out, the family departed their war-torn homeland for America and 97 Orchard Street.

It was a miserable letdown: seven people crammed into the top-floor apartment, wash publicly hung from their fire escape and rats infested the building. New York was especially trying for the 30,000 Sephardic Jews who came from North African and Middle Eastern countries. The Sephardim, whose ancestors had fled persecution in Spain and Portugal, had different customs and spoke a Hebrew-Spanish mix called Ladino, which set them apart from their Yiddish-speaking neighbors.

Abraham soon found work as a pushcart peddler and by 1916 this determined loner owned an underwear factory on Allen Street. Rachel, a sweet, sociable woman, took care of the children (she bore between 13 and 18 children, but only eight survived childhood) and enjoyed smoking cigarettes and playing poker.

In the tenement's front room, the Confino's remaining daughter Victoria, slept on the bed, while their five sons slept on crates with thick Turkish rugs called mantas. In 1915, Abraham also briefly took in two nephews. The lively and sharp-tongued Victoria protested being removed from school at 13 to work in her father's factory and she became bitter when her mother made her scrub floors on her lunch hour. Like her sister, Allegra, she later resented being forced into an arranged marriage.

Joseph worked first as a tinsmith before joining the family business. While his brothers Jacob, Salvatore and Saul became throughly American and took new names—Jack, Charlie and Bob—Joseph remained traditional and religious. Brother David truly rebelled: he went to college and convinced his siblings, except Joseph, to change their surname to Coffield. David's children weren't given a Jewish upbringing, although in the 1930s, he helped found the Broome and Allen Street Boys, a Sephardic organization that raised money to send poor kids to camp.

The Confinos moved from 97 Orchard Street to East Harlem around 1916, though Abraham arranged for a nephew, Joseph, to move into the tenement that same year. While Joseph and his wife, Sarah, both immigrants, only stayed for two years, they remained fixtures in the neighborhood, founding Fit-Rite Dresses on Allen Street, which they operated from the 1920s until 1970.

The art was especially refreshing since the addition of gas lights the previous decade had exposed the true nature of these cheerless foyers. All these new touches gave the aging tenement a much-needed boost at a time when it was competing with more modern "New Law" tenements in the neighborhood.

These minor attempts to upgrade the building were not enough to satisfy social reformers who highlighted the ramshackle, spiritless quality of tenements in order to galvanize public support for much-needed regulation.

THREE

While the apartments were small and primitive, they weren't generally overcrowded at first. In 1870, 71 people lived in the building. Ninety-Seven Orchard Street was home to working-class immigrants and many were artisans and skilled laborers: a musician, a jeweler, a maker of surgical instruments. While there were Irish laborers, and a handful of Russians and Austrians, most residents were German Protestants or Catholics, from Prussia or Bavaria. And although they were new to the country, many had registered to fight in the Union Army shortly after moving into the building in 1864. By 1890, startling surges in immigration had transformed the neighborhood. The tenement now housed 110 people, an average of two extra people in each tiny apartment. Russian, Austrian, Polish and Romanian Jews replaced German Protestants and Catholics. By the turn of the century, only two Germans remained.

Overcrowding in the tenements hit a high point by the turn of the century. Eight people in one apartment was not uncommon.

Most adults spoke Yiddish.

The building was increasingly overcrowded. In 1900, three apartments housed eight people each and one was home to nine; 13 residents were lodgers, living mostly with the poorest and largest families. Most of the immigrants now toiled in the garment industry as shirt-makers, pant-makers, suspender-makers and peddlers.

Newcomers moved out of this pre-"Old Law" tenement as soon as they could. The constant turnover brought new cultures into 97 Orchard Street — among the 102 residents in 1915 were 16 Ladino-speaking Sephardic Jews fleeing revolution in what is today northern Greece.

Immigration slowed during World War I, and virtually halted after Congress "shut the Golden Door" with restrictive quotas in the 1920s. With few new immigrants replacing those who had moved away, the Lower East Side was no longer as packed with people. By 1925, life at 97 Orchard Street had again changed drastically. Only 12 of the building's households were occupied, but the families — who now came in equal numbers from Turkey, Greece, Russia, Spain and Austria — remained poor and large, with seven or eight people often crammed into an apartment.

The Baldizzis and other Italian Catholics present in 1935 make it clear that the tenement's populace continued evolving until the residents were evicted. Had the apartments remained open, today they would likely be filled with Asian and Hispanic immigrants.

Adolpho Baldizzi c. 1917, before emigrating to New York.

THE BALDIZZIS

Adolfo Baldizzi had heard stories that the streets of America were paved with gold. So, in 1923, this skilled cabinetmaker from Palermo, Italy stowed away on a ship, only to end up on the Lower East Side, where the streets were dirty and cluttered. Undeterred, Baldizzi brought his young wife Rosaria over a year later, and on Elizabeth Street, surrounded by fellow Sicilians, they started a family.

In 1928, behind on their rent, the family simply moved to another nearby tenement, 97 Orchard Street. Their home was poorly heated and barely furnished with one regular bed, one metal fold-up bed for two-year-old Josephine and baby John, a bureau, a table and a trunk. During the Great Depression Adolfo was reduced to walking the streets with his toolbox, looking for odd jobs. Rosaria, who lined coats in a garment factory, had to quit because her meager paycheck endangered the family's Home Relief check. When they had spending money, Adolfo treated the kids to nickel root beers, charlotte russes, and potato pancakes on Essex Street. He entertained them with riddles and games of Chinese checkers and tic-tac-toe while Rosaria listened to Italian operas on the radio.

Allen Street, c.1938.

Rosaria Baldizzi in the 1930s.

With most relatives in Italy, neighbors like the Bonfiglios, Raspizzios, and Dragos became extended family. The Baldizzis also mingled easily with the tenement's Jewish families. On Fridays, Josephine dutifully turned on the lights for her neighbors, the Rosenthals, who were prohibited by Jewish law from working on the Sabbath. "I felt so proud that they chose me for this," recalled Josephine.

In 1935, this community of immigrants and their children was suddenly broken up. While the building's businesses were allowed to stay open, every family at 97 Orchard Street was evicted.

The Baldizzis and several other families moved to Eldridge Street and later to Brooklyn. But Adolfo and Rosaria kept shopping on Orchard Street, as did Josephine a generation later. When the Lower East Side Tenement Museum opened more than a half-century later, Josephine was among the pioneers who helped ease the Museum staff into 97 Orchard Street and made them feel right at home.

Today's immigrants, like their predecessors, are transforming the neighborhood — and challenging us to provide new answers to old questions. Who is American? What does it mean to be a citizen? What is our responsibility to those in need? What should "home" look like? It is their future that gives the past — a past that this Museum studies and celebrates — such resonance.

opposite, Allen Street today with tenement housing still in use.

below, A former public bathhouse now serves the latest wave of Asian immigrants as The Church of Grace of the Fujianese, New York.

PROFESSIONAL
COMPUTER
Microwise International
電 COMPUTER
Resale Service & Wholesale
CABLING
華洋地毯公司
3房高级地毯 $300
地毯、底胶、人工
300平方呎
INDOOR OUTDOOR
FLOORING SUPPLIES
Scotchgard
Luxura
105 Allen St.
Tel: 219-8772

Fortune Teller, Chinatown, 1992.

Clinton Street, 1987.

credits

Front cover image © Joel Cohen
p 10 left: Ellis Island Museum of Immigration
right: The New York Public Library
p 20 left: Polly Garagosian
right: Benjamin Trimmier
p 25: The New-York Historical Society
p 27: Courtesy of Angela Voulangas
pp 29, 30: Museum of the City of New York
p 33: Courtesy of the Community Service Society
p 35, 37: Marlis Momber
p 36: Angela Voulangas
p 38: The New York Public Library
p 39: National Archives
p 49: Courtesy of Julia Della Croce
p 51: The Municipal Archives of the City of New York
p 53: Angela Voulangas
p 54: © Andrew Garn
p 55: Ted Barron

All other images are from the collection of the Lower East Side Tenement Museum.

The cover incorporates images of some of the textures and building materials found at 97 Orchard Street. Shown are pressed tin, wall coverings, c. 1900-1920, wood lathing, and layers of paint c. 1930s.

The Museum extends special thanks to Mort Sheinman. He served as the editor of the 2004 publication, shaping and trimming the new language to create a seamless and engaging revision. He generously donated his time and energy to the Tenement Museum.

STUART MILLER is the co-author, with Sharon Seitz, of "The Other Islands of New York City: A Historical Companion" (The Countryman Press). He was also a contributing writer to "City Guide: New York" (Alfred Knopf), and has written about the city for *Esquire*, *New York* Magazine, the *New York Times Magazine*, the *Daily News*, *Newsday*, and *Time Out New York*.

ANGELA VOULANGAS helped shape *A Tenement Story*. She is a freelance writer and graphic designer who buys too many books about New York history.

REVEALING THE PAST. CHALLENGING THE FUTURE.